g So Long Bother!
eople U
Wolves
'm Scar
or Life
People's Minds . . . and They
Up Alone Holy Shit Did I Turn
o List Is Kicking My Ass I Thin
wkward Meeting People I Cr
tchup I Need to Proofread Tex
g It's Too Late to Change Care
j, I Might Eat All the Bread O
y Not That Talented Ugh, Wh
h? I'm Nothing Without [ins
ot This (or That) (or That oth
Bad Choice, Ever I Get Thro
Shit! Pretty Much Everything
's Only Going to Get Worse!
lk I'm Afraid to Speak Up WH
Getting Older? Once I Get t
rfect I'm Too Busy for Self-C
rything Perfectly Perfectly!
I Want to Be Good at Stuff—

Created and published by Knock Knock
6695 Green Valley Circle, #5167
Culver City, CA 90230
knockknockstuff.com

Illustrations © Peter Arkle

This book is a work of humorous nonfiction meant solely for entertainment
purposes. It is not intended to be an actual therapist or magic fix-it pill.
In no event will Knock Knock be liable to any reader for any damages,
including direct, indirect, incidental, special, consequential, or punitive,
arising out of or in connection to the information contained in this book.
If we got something factually wrong, tell us so we can correct it in
subsequent editions. If you don't end up letting go of shit—it's not our fault.
But we really hope you do!

Every reasonable attempt has been made to identify owners of copyright.
Errors or omissions will be corrected in subsequent editions.

Where specific company, product, and brand names are cited, copyright
and trademarks associated with these names are property of their
respective owners.

ISBN: 978-1-68349-378-5
UPC: 8-25703-50126-1
10 9 8 7 6 5 4 3 2 1

LET GO OF THAT SH*T

Anxiety
Stress
Catastrophizing

KNOCK
KNOCK®
LOS ANGELES, CALIFORNIA

Contents

INTRODUCTION

IF YOU'RE LIKE MOST PEOPLE, YOUR LIFE IS JAMMED WITH SHIT THAT STRESSES YOU OUT. Career issues, endless tasks and errands, relationships, social anxieties, hopes and dreams ...The shit list is endless! No wonder your poor brain feels overwhelmed and overheated, like an oven stuck on "broil" ...your entire nervous system is positively inflamed with stress. It's exhausting!

Trouble is, you've been in chronic worry-about-everything mode for so long, it feels familiar, almost like it's protecting you from an even worse fate. Who knows what might happen if you relaxed your anxiety muscles a bit and let your guard down? Things might REALLY fall apart, ya know?

This book gets it. Each short entry expresses the kind of mental chatter lots of us live with every day, giving voice to fears, anxieties, and insecurities in all their dramatic glory—and then answering them with comforting, commonsense clapbacks! The idea is to reframe your fears and foibles in a more positive, forgiving light... and give your anxiety-addled mind a rest. Oh, and to laugh.

Each entry also includes a little tear-out slip for you to write on and then release. Make a ritual out of it! Light a candle! Bury it, burn it, or flush it down the toilet!

Let go of that sh*t.

There Aren't Enough Hours in the Day So Why Bother?

LOOKING AROUND THE CHAOS OF YOUR HOME, you wonder: How do people with jobs (or kids, or just social lives) ALSO manage to do the dishes every day? And the laundry? And tidy up? And water the plants? And buy toilet paper? And throw out unidentifiable items from the back of the fridge? And pay the cable bill? You think about these things for a while. And then you decide to lie on the couch and watch a little more TV.

LET GO OF THAT SHIT!

OK, so these are the universal and incessant questions of the modern era. You are officially forbidden to beat yourself up about this type of bullshit. But solutions-wise, here's an idea: Maybe you should try to de-focus on the big picture—ALL the things you need to do—and try zooming in on one task? Say, the sink full of dishes. If you can do one small thing, you will feel less overwhelmed—it literally never fails.

NOPE, NOT TODAY, SHIT!
I HEREBY OFFICIALLY RELEASE YOU!

Initials: _____

Date: _____

SHITTY WORRY NO. **2**

I Feel Like a Huge Weirdo in a World of Normal People

PERHAPS YOU FEEL LIKE everyone else in the world belongs to a secret Everyone-Else Club, and they meet to talk about important secret things, and also talk about YOU. Or maybe you are someone who walks into a party and assumes everyone there went to high school together, and you've got no chance of fitting in...and that even if you had known them in high school, you still would have felt like an outsider!

LET GO OF THAT SHIT!

So many of us feel this way (most of us?). You may be an introvert or highly sensitive person who isn't suited to crowds. But that's not something that you need to "fix." It's part of your magic and your personal power. Tons of successful people are wired that way. BTW, there's no Everyone-Else Club—or if there is, we're not members, either. So fuck 'em!

NOPE. NOT TODAY, SHIT!
I HEREBY OFFICIALLY RELEASE YOU!
Initials: _____ Date: _____

Ugh. I'm So Lazy!

YOU KNOW HOW TO WORK HARD AND GET THINGS DONE, but there are days (and sometimes weeks) when you just CAN'T. DO. ANYTHING. You can waste hours on the couch, watching TV, exploring internet rabbit holes, or just puttering around the house, muttering to yourself. There are days when you valiantly try to focus, sometimes for hours, and get less than nothing done (which is, admittedly, a scientific marvel!).

LET GO OF THAT SHIT!

We all need days to recharge. Like, even Superman retreats to his Fortress of Solitude! Some days, that might look like being "lazy" on the surface. But what if things are actually just percolating behind the scenes? What if your subconscious mind is just low-key busy solving problems like how to quit the job you hate, trick your kids into eating broccoli, and achieve world peace? By the way, you're doing fine.

NOPE. NOT TODAY, SHIT!

I HEREBY OFFICIALLY RELEASE YOU!

Initials: _____

Date: _____

I'm Bad at Parties

ANOTHER PARTY INVITATION? WHY? More small talk. More people playing the acoustic guitar. More eating tiny food off of tiny plates. More awkward moments looking around for someone to talk to...while also trying to avoid being someone other people think looks approachable. How long before you can slip out? Will there be a dog to play with? Ugh. The party hasn't even started and it's already too much work.

LET GO OF THAT SHIT!

Bad at parties? Maybe. Skilled at the art of enjoying your own company? Hells yeah! That's a genuine superpower—one that many people will never master, and that will serve you well for your entire life. So there. Also, you're probably not as bad at parties as you think you are. Either way, it's OK to be shy. It's OK to be a wallflower, even. You can be the intriguing and mysterious guest—every good party needs at least one of those.

NOPE. NOT TODAY, SHIT!

I HEREBY OFFICIALLY RELEASE YOU!

Initials: _____

Date: _____

I Might Be Attacked by Wolves, or Something!

OR COYOTES. OR, IF YOU'RE CAMPING, A BEAR or mountain lion or even a rabid racoon. Hey, THESE THINGS HAPPEN. Did you know people get killed by owls? Or there could be an earthquake, nuclear bomb, zombies, plane crash. Your family could move out while you're at the dentist getting a surprise root canal. Face it, you're doomed.

LET GO OF THAT SHIT!

Welp. Technically, you're not wrong. Crazy shit happens! But just because some people have actually been killed by falling debris from space doesn't mean it's not safe to go outside. Panic mode is no fun! If you're worried about surprise root canals, just take better care of your teeth. And maybe consider learning to meditate?

NOPE. NOT TODAY, SHIT!

I HEREBY OFFICIALLY RELEASE YOU!

Initials: _____

Date: _____

SHITTY WORRY | NO. 6

I'm Too Old to Start Living My #Bestlife

YOU HAVE SO MANY GREAT SKILLS AND QUALITIES, but one thing is not on your side: time. It waits for no one (except maybe J. Lo). And unfortunately, you've kinda frittered your best years on not-quite-right relationships, career tangents, TV, and general farting around. And now you're really getting up there! If you tried to take up a new life pursuit or dream at this point, it would just be kind of sad and embarrassing.

LET GO OF THAT SHIT!

You need to take this in with a quickness: if you're alive, it's not too late to kick ass. Seriously. If anyone thinks it's sad or embarrassing, um, SO WHAT? You won't die of embarrassment. Using age as an excuse to deny yourself what you really want is a form of procrastination. Need gumption? Binge-watch YouTube videos about 70-year-old weightlifters and 99-year-old ballerinas until you find some! Time's gonna pass whether you live fully or not. So go get 'em, appropriately-aged tiger.

NOPE. NOT TODAY, SHIT!

I HEREBY OFFICIALLY RELEASE YOU!

Initials: _____

Date: _____

I'm Afraid of Losing People

MAYBE THE PANIC HITS YOU AT 3 A.M., or maybe it's a chronic, low-level unease, like background static. But it's there: worry about losing people you love. It's scary and it sucks, and it makes you feel powerless. And the more love and joy you have, the more fear you have. UGH. Aren't love and happiness supposed to make you...happy?

LET GO OF THAT SHIT!

Profound love often brings the fear of loss. Totally normal! But it is possible to be happy *and* aware of the reality that we're all mortal. Some people even find that this awareness makes life feel more rich. In any case, ruminating about future loss will not magically protect your future heart. It won't protect your loved ones from their own mortality. It won't make anyone happy. And have you ever heard of someone on their deathbed saying, "Gee, I wish I hadn't loved so much. I wish I had worried MORE."?

NOPE. NOT TODAY, SHIT!
I HEREBY OFFICIALLY RELEASE YOU!
Initials: _____
Date: _____

SHITTY WORRY | NO. 8

I'm Kinda Scared of Success

SOMETIMES YOU WORRY about what might happen if, gasp, you actually got the success, recognition, and material rewards you desire (and deserve!). Would you lose your safe, cozy anonymity? Would you get trolled by haters? Would you be expected to repeat your success, again and again? You might lose the freedom to make mistakes! You might get a big head! Worst of all, you'll be found out.

LET GO OF THAT SHIT!

OR! OR! OR! What if you find new dreams to dream after you accomplish the first few? What if you have no haters, just people genuinely happy for your success? What if you find new things to be good at, while still being successful with what you did before? What if life just keeps getting better and better? You're not from the future...you have no idea all of the good things that could be in store for you!

NOPE. NOT TODAY, SHIT!

I HEREBY OFFICIALLY RELEASE YOU!

Initials: _____

Date: _____

SHITTY WORRY | NO. **9**

I Make Poor Life Choices

BUT, BUT, BUT... cutting your own bangs after getting dumped and drinking a bottle of wine seemed like a really good plan at the time! And buying that super cool 1970s Porsche you couldn't afford and never actually got running? Still looks fantastic sitting in your driveway! So there. Oh and sure, rent is late but you really deserve some cool new shoes and a weekend in the country... It's been such a hard week/month/year!

LET GO OF THAT SHIT!

Show us someone who hasn't made bad decisions and we'll show you a robot. A really boring robot. The fact that you acknowledge your errors and feel bad about them means you're not a robot— or a psychopathic narcissist. So there. Now giddy-up, you beautiful mess!

NOPE. NOT TODAY, SHIT!
I HEREBY OFFICIALLY RELEASE YOU!
Initials: _____
Date: _____

I'm Turning Into a Hopeless Scatterbrain

YOU'RE A LOOOONG WAY FROM BEING "OLD,"
but you've been misplacing your keys or phone or
water bottle (a lot). You forget birthdays. You can never
remember the names of actors (or writers, movies,
books, dogs, kids)...And you totally spaced a doctor
visit. You could tie a string around your finger, but there's
a 50/50 chance you'd just look at it later and go,
"What's this doing here?"

LET GO OF THAT SHIT!

In the age of smartphones and laptops, we're force-fed
constant information, which means our hard drives—
er, memory banks—fill up faster. People in Jane Austen's
time would marvel at the info-tsunami our brains process
daily. Stress, hormone changes, and sleep issues don't
help. You're very normal! You can turn off your phone.
You can meditate. And good for you—you're reading an
actual paper book!

NOPE. NOT TODAY, SHIT!

I HEREBY OFFICIALLY RELEASE YOU!

Initials: _____

Date: _____

I Can Read People's Minds... and They're Thinking Bad Things

YOU HAVE A SECRET POWER: You can hear people's thoughts! OK, maybe not literally HEAR them, but you definitely know what they're thinking, because you're perceptive and, yes, a tiny bit omniscient. You can easily interpret a nod from your boss or a two-word text from a friend. That's how you know that most people are kind of mad at you right now. They're annoyed, and they think you're boring and uncool. The other people aren't mad at you—just disappointed. Being telepathic is a blessing and a curse!

LET GO OF THAT SHIT!

There's some good news and some bad news. The bad news is, you can't read people's minds. The good news is, YOU CAN'T READ PEOPLE'S MINDS. Roughly 89 percent of the time, other people are thinking about their own insecurities and worrying that everyone else is kind of mad at them. So based on statistics, you can go ahead and proceed as if you are generally liked, and maybe consider that the other person could use a friendly wave or high five or something.

NOPE. NOT TODAY, SHIT!
I HEREBY OFFICIALLY RELEASE YOU!
Initials: _____
Date: _____

I'm Gonna End Up Alone

SOMETIMES YOU LIE AWAKE AT NIGHT staring into the darkness, contemplating the possibility that you may never meet The One, that special person who will stay with you until the very end like in *The Notebook*. You find your mind spinning, imagining a bleak and shabby bedroom in the future, where an older you lies alone, reaching out for a hand to hold...but no one is there. You, yes you, are all alone!

LET GO OF THAT SHIT!

Well, that COULD happen...but it's highly unlikely. You may be single, but chances are very good that you will have people around who care about you. And that's a very different thing from being "alone." It's actually the opposite of being alone. Another thing to consider: lots of people discover in their senior years that they actually enjoy being single.

NOPE. NOT TODAY, SHIT!

I HEREBY OFFICIALLY RELEASE YOU!

Initials: _____

Date: _____

SHITTY WORRY NO. **13**

Holy Shit Did I Turn Off the Oven?

TEN MINUTES AFTER LEAVING HOME you have a terrible thought: Did I leave the oven on? Did I lock the door? Did I close the door? What about that window—did I close it? And what about the iron, and the toaster, and possibly the shower? Is my home going to be robbed, burned down, and flooded today—all because I forgot to turn things off? Yes, obviously. All that stuff is going to happen. Plus, a tornado.

LET GO OF THAT SHIT!

Let's get real about this common human behavior: it's a mind trick! Your brain feels overwhelmed and to compensate, it's trying to get you to slow down. It's actually kind of clever, if intensely annoying. These thoughts are speedbumps intended to prevent you from moving forward with your day. So thank your brain for trying to protect you—and then move on! If you did leave your window open, think of all the fresh air you'll come home to.

NOPE. NOT TODAY, SHIT!

I HEREBY OFFICIALLY RELEASE YOU!

Initials: _____

Date: _____

My Super Awesome To-Do List Is Kicking My Ass

YOU'RE EXTREMELY COMPETENT AND HAVE MAD SKILLS in many departments. You often juggle five (or twelve!) things at once, and you sacrifice your own sleep and/or sanity in order to maintain your A+ standards. When it comes to getting shit done, it's quality *and* quantity, people!

LET GO OF THAT SHIT!

So what if you're not the best at time management? Being time-optimistic is not crime. Buuuut also: Your time is a non-renewable energy source. Maybe consider your priorities: Is there a way to spend more time on stuff you really, really care about, and give less of your time/sleep/essential life force to the other stuff? Yes. The answer is yes. Juggling is overrated, btw (unless it's like knives or fire and you're in Cirque du Soleil or something).

NOPE. NOT TODAY, SHIT!
I HEREBY OFFICIALLY RELEASE YOU!
Initials: _____
Date: _____

I Think I Might Be Boring?

DO YOU EVER STEP BACK AND LOOK AT YOURSELF and think, um, when did I get so *basic*? When you meet someone and share the thumbnail version of your life, do you feel like they're stifling yawns? Everything from your car to your favorite TV show quietly announces your epic Average Jane-ness (or Average Joe-ness). The world of self-help books and influencers keeps telling you to be more YOU, be DIFFERENT, stand out! But they actually don't offer a ton of specific advice if the "real you" is really a little boring.

LET GO OF THAT SHIT!

Vanilla ice cream gets lots of grief for being boring, bland, and average. But guess what? It's super good, and goes really well with other flavors. It's the most popular ice cream in the universe. So what does "average" *mean*? By whose yardstick are you average? Because rest assured, even Lady Gaga has her completely boring aspects. Sometimes it's OK to find yourself in the middle. It's OK to just do what you need or want to do, and save the epic striving for later. On average, you're a pretty cool and inherently interesting person.

NOPE. NOT TODAY, SHIT!
I HEREBY OFFICIALLY RELEASE YOU!
Initials: _____
Date: _____

I Am Just Super Awkward Meeting People

YOU HAD A TOILET-SEAT COVER STUCK TO YOUR SHOE. You snorted (LOUD) while laughing. You were late and then got their name wrong (twice). You got weird and awkward and overshared with poppy seeds in your teeth. First impressions stick. Yep, you're now forever THAT person.

LET GO OF THAT SHIT!

Ever heard of a second chance? They exist for a reason, and it's only natural they'd come along sometime *after* a first impression. We all get do-overs in life. We can give them to ourselves, and grant them to other people. Also, sometimes doing something dumb or awkward can be endearing—or at least good for a laugh down the line?

NOPE. NOT TODAY, SHIT!
I HEREBY OFFICIALLY RELEASE YOU!

Initials: _____

Date: _____

I Crave Approval Like French Fries Crave Ketchup

AS A KID, YOU BASKED IN PRAISE from parents, teachers, random old ladies at the supermarket. What an *adorable*, *polite*, *smart*, [etc.!] little child you were! It felt so warm and safe to be in the good graces of adults—to be the favorite, the teacher's pet. As an adult, you still want validation, permission, full-throated cheerleading for stuff, and if you don't get it you feel like a loser. Sometimes you give up on things you wanted to do. But hey, you probably would have flopped anyway!

LET GO OF THAT SHIT!

You know the old phrase "everyone's a critic"? In the age of social media it's doubly true. Our society lives to rate and judge people, places, and tacos. We even carry a machine in our pockets that lets us instantly broadcast our opinions. No doubt this human foible is here to stay. (In future, people will probably rate space hotels—"★ ★ OK, not as nice as the ones in Sector C7-49B.") But to not go crazy, maybe pick a handful of people whose opinions matter to you—and fuck the rest. Nicely.

NOPE. NOT TODAY, SHIT!

I HEREBY OFFICIALLY RELEASE YOU!

Initials: _____ Date: _____

I Need to Proofread Texts & Emails a Million Times Before Sending

APPARENTLY, THERE ARE PEOPLE IN THE WORLD who send texts and emails, and leave messages, without wasting psychic energy on how they will be perceived. They don't lose sleep over the odd typo, or fear getting fired if the tone of their email isn't EXACTLY PERFECTLY JUST SO. WTF, people? Don't they care about details? Don't they fear public shaming for making accidentally typing two periods at the end of a sentence?

LET GO OF THAT SHIT!

When you get a text with a typo, do you cut that person out of your life? If you get an awkward voice mail, do you mock it as you play it for your friends? When you get a work email, do you comb through it hunting for errors, and forward it to your boss with the mistakes highlighted? No; that would be weird! Generally, if a person is nice and competent, people kinda overlook their tiny mistakes. Everyone makes 'em. So maybe you can offer yourself the same grace! Just to prove it, here's a typoo...

NOPE. NOT TODAY, SHIT!
I HEREBY OFFICIALLY RELEASE YOU!
Initials: _____
Date: _____

SHITTY WORRY | NO. **19**

It's Too Late to Change Careers

WHY DID YOU WASTE SO MUCH TIME ON THE WRONG THINGS? Like ... your job. If you tried to make a career change now, you'd be wasting all that time and money you spent getting educated and trained and promoted in your current job. Plus, you'd have to start all over again at the bottom somewhere new, and there's no guarantee that you would end up liking your new job. If you try and turn a passion into a job, it could kill your passion! Here you are, already getting by just fine, and it's the devil you know, so why risk it all now?

LET GO OF THAT SHIT!

Your life is like a really cool, crazy tapestry, and you're always working on it. Tweaking, changing, enhancing it. Your past experiences are never "wasted." They glint like golden threads in your tapestry ... and emerald green, and scarlet. The more the better! If you make a career change and wind up hating it, guess what? You can switch again. Go back to your old career. Or try a new one. Whoever has the coolest tapestry at the end wins!

NOPE. NOT TODAY, SHIT!

I HEREBY OFFICIALLY RELEASE YOU!

Initials: _____

Date: _____

My Parents Messed Me Up

FACTS: YOU DIDN'T RAISE YOU—YOUR PARENTS DID. And by golly did they do a number on you! If it wasn't for them, you'd be a totally different human. You might not be taller or have better teeth (because genetics), but you'd be different, probably a whole lot more [insert all the good things] and a whole lot less [insert all the bad things]. If only they hadn't gotten their hands on you first!

LET GO OF THAT SHIT!

It's true—it's all true! But then again, you could've had even worse parents. (Hey, anything is possible!) In the end, it comes down to this: owning your own shit is liberating. That's kinda how healing starts. Think of it as a power move! And if you need to, consider the gift that they gave you as anti-role models: showing you all the things you don't want to be. Your awesomeness is partly due to their bad example!

NOPE. NOT TODAY, SHIT!

I HEREBY OFFICIALLY RELEASE YOU!

Initials: _____

Date: _____

SHITTY WORRY — NO. 21

Someday, I Might Eat All the Bread

MAYBE YOU'RE INVOLVED IN A LONG-TERM AFFAIR WITH BREAD. Or cheese. Or candy. Maybe French fries are your Achilles' heel. You try to resist 'em, but you just can't quit 'em, because you're weak-willed, ravenous, and possibly immoral! And if you continue down this path of indulgence and gluttony, who knows? Maybe one day you will wind up eating all the bread (or pizza, candy, etc.) in the world, and float away like a balloon.

LET GO OF THAT SHIT!

The reason you can't quit the foods you love isn't that you're weak and gluttonous—it's that your love is true. Time to bring this affair out into the open and proclaim it to the world! And unless your doctor says otherwise, there's no reason to quit. Just maybe mix in some salads and get in some long walks.

NOPE. NOT TODAY, SHIT!

I HEREBY OFFICIALLY RELEASE YOU!

Initials: _____

Date: _____

Oof, I Said the Dumbest Thing

REMEMBER THAT DUMB THING YOU SAID THAT ONE TIME that you can't let go of? Of course you do. How could you ever forget? It was super dumb! And it made you look super dumb, and like a huge, stupid jerk. People are still whispering about it behind your back. No one will ever forget it. Your tombstone will probably read, "Here Lies That Person Who Said That Dumb Thing That One Time."

LET GO OF THAT SHIT!

Universal Human Truth: We think about ourselves way more than other people think about us. After all, they're too busy thinking about themselves to be thinking about you. it's highly likely no one even remembers what you said and even if they do, they're probably thinking about other dumb things other not-dumb people have said in the meantime. Yay!

NOPE. NOT TODAY, SHIT!
I HEREBY OFFICIALLY RELEASE YOU!

Initials: _____

Date: _____

SHITTY WORRY | NO. **23**

I'm Really Not That Talented

YOU KNOW THAT LITTLE VOICE INSIDE YOUR HEAD? The one that says things to you like: "Who do you think you are?" And maybe something like: "You're not the sun, dumb dumb, so stop shining!" That little voice that says that what you have to offer the world isn't good enough, and you should hide your talent under a bush or something like that? That voice sucks, but surely it's that loud/confident/ determined for a reason, right?!

LET GO OF THAT SHIT!

That little voice IS the worst, but the good news is, that voice is full of shit. It's not protecting you. It's making you scared to unfurl your freak flag and fully inhabit your creative space in the world. Listen, when you don't share your gifts with the world, you are essentially robbing the world of something only you can offer. Are you a criminal? Didn't think so!

NOPE. NOT TODAY, SHIT!
I HEREBY OFFICIALLY RELEASE YOU!
Initials: _____
Date: _____

Ugh, What If I Have to Start Over from Scratch?

WHETHER YOU BURN A BATCH OF COOKIES
or your life just sort of explodes all over the place,
starting over from scratch is such a slog! Even
contemplating it is exhausting. Where would you even
start? Like, what if you lost your job, or your relationship,
or your home? (Hey, hurricanes and wildfires and
earthquakes HAPPEN!) What if your professional skills
became obsolete? What if someone stole your identity
and emptied your bank account? The possibilities of
things that could go wrong are infinite!

LET GO OF THAT SHIT!

OK, OK, these things do happen. Everyone experiences
all kinds of loss, and yes, starting over is daunting.
But you never start over 100% from scratch, because
every time you start over, you have more experience
and wisdom than the last time (and, possibly, more
professional contacts and skills). Plus, starting over
can be glorious. So weird, right? It's a fresh start,
a reboot, a do-over, and an opportunity to have,
do, or be what you really want. It's a chance
to be true to you. Just channel Bob in *What
About Bob?* "Oh, boy! Baby steps, baby
steps. Baby steps through the office.
Baby steps out the door. It works.
It works." Bob gets it.

NOPE. NOT TODAY, SHIT!

I HEREBY OFFICIALLY RELEASE YOU!

Initials: _____

Date: _____

I'm Nothing Without [Insert Whatever Thing Here]!

WHEN YOU WERE A KID, you didn't define yourself by external things like work, hobbies, politics, religion, whatever. You were just...YOU. And that was enough! So how did you wind up where you are today, with your self-esteem so fragile and your sense of identity so tied up in your job? Or your family? Or your [insert thing here]? It's like your identity is a big jenga set, and if one piece got pulled out too fast—TIMBER!

LET GO OF THAT SHIT!

It's human nature to define ourselves by our social and family roles—and also, in our capitalist society, by things like our job title, paycheck, and productivity. It's super hard—maybe impossible—not to lose ourselves a bit in that bullshit. But it is kinda bullshit. 'Cause you have inherent value that is so huge it can't be measured at all. You did as a kid—you do now. You exist. Even if you lose your job or your house or your faith or your Twitter following!

NOPE. NOT TODAY, SHIT!

I HEREBY OFFICIALLY RELEASE YOU!

Initials: _____

Date: _____

I So Don't Got This (or That) (or That Other Thing)

FUUUUCK...IT'S ALL TOO MUCH, this "adulting" shit. You're running late, always. You blew a deadline or forgot to pay a bill (yikes!). You're way underqualified and probably not smart enough (you've just fooled them!). You've dropped the ball with friendships and personal commitments—but it's just too much pressure. Argh! No one should count on you. Including you.

LET GO OF THAT SHIT!

Easy there. Maybe you feel like you're dropping balls like a gumball machine at a Chuck E. Cheese. But it's not because you're dumb or bad or flaky. You are (generally) on time! You have good ideas, you're super smart, you make good choices, and you're absolutely qualified! You've got a good-enough memory, and you can start writing things down more! Right now, you're just in a stress spiral. Focus on the stress. Fix THAT. Not YOU. You don't need fixing.

NOPE. NOT TODAY, SHIT!

I HEREBY OFFICIALLY RELEASE YOU!

Initials: _____

Date: _____

I Never Ever Want to Make a Bad Choice, Ever

UM, IF YOU'RE NOT SWEATING THE SMALL STUFF (AND the big stuff) who will? That stuff ain't gonna sweat itself. And sweat you do, whether it's choosing a pair of sneakers, picking out paint colors, or quitting your day job and starting a vegan donut truck. 'Cause who knows what might happen if you make the wrong choice? The Earth could spin off its axis, causing a new ice age and mass devastation. Vegan donuts could get cancelled. You never know!

LET GO OF THAT SHIT!

You're awesome and powerful, for sure, but you're not, like, THAT kind of powerful. You won't cause major planetary climate events because you try a new job. (Unless your new job is being a mad supervillain with a Secret Weather Machine of Doom.) Most of the time, things aren't set in stone. You can change your mind and make a new choice if the first choice doesn't work out. In fact, those do-overs are kind of awesome. The do-over zone is where a lot of the best stuff in life happens. Plus donuts—even vegan ones— are forevs.

NOPE. NOT TODAY, SHIT!
I HEREBY OFFICIALLY RELEASE YOU!
Initials: _____ Date: _____

SHITTY WORRY | NO. **28**

I Get Thrown Off-Balance by Change—Even Tiny Shit!

HAVE YOU STAYED IN BORING, UNHAPPY, OR OTHERWISE UNSATISFACTORY RELATIONSHIPS because you didn't want the upheaval of a breakup? Or stuck it out in dumb jobs for the same reason? Maybe you get stressed out by any last-minute change of plans or tweaks to your routine. (Why are other people are always trying to switch things up, anyway?) You might like to try living abroad for a year...but it'd be such a huge disruption. Better to just stay here in the same-old same-old...same-old.

LET GO OF THAT SHIT!

Being a creature of habit is not a mortal sin. Change is scary and disruptive and hard. The status quo exists for a reason! There's a time and place for the venerable status quo! But there's also a time for change, whether by choice or fate. Change contains a gift: the chance to make a new choice. That can be very fun and surprising—or lead you to listen to your gut and make a better choice. Fortunately, most changes are not totally un-do-over-able. Those bangs will definitely grow out.

NOPE, NOT TODAY, SHIT!

I HEREBY OFFICIALLY RELEASE YOU!

Initials: _____ Date: _____

Pretty Much Everything Is My Fault

YOU HAVE A HABIT OF SAYING SORRY A LOT, even for things like a coworker getting a papercut— things that seemingly aren't your fault. But you know better, because you know that secretly, mysteriously, everything is totally your fault. That includes big things and little things. Global warming. WWII. Clumpy mascara. Nickelback. When someone else bumps into you or cuts you off in traffic . . . Yep, it's all on you. Your bad.

LET GO OF THAT SHIT!

Sometimes guilt is OK if it spurs you towards positive action. But lots of the time it just makes us feel like shit and demoralizes us into inaction. Oh, and by the way: You are not individually responsible for WWII (or any other war), or global warming, or historical crimes against humanity. You ARE responsible for Nickelback, however. (KIDDING.)

NOPE. NOT TODAY, SHIT!

I HEREBY OFFICIALLY RELEASE YOU!

Initials: _____

Date: _____

Ack...
I'm Lonely,
and
It's Only
Going to
Get Worse!

SOMETIMES YOU FEEL WEIRDLY ALONE...
even when you're not alone. And then especially when
you are alone. Maybe you'll always be lonely? Maybe
no one will ever love you enough to stick with you
through thick and thin. Maybe you're a people-repellent
person, and you smell weird—but you'll never know,
because you'll always be alone alone alone, except for
the lonely little cricket who plays his violin in the night
outside your lonely window!

LET GO OF THAT SHIT!

All kidding aside, loneliness hurts. The (kinda) good
news ... you're not alone in feeling alone. (Oh, the
irony!) Most people feel lonelier than ever. Some real
smart people (from Harvard!) are even researching this
crazy "loneliness epidemic" and its effects. There's
no magic pill for it—yet—but there IS now a whole
institute called The Unlonely Project devoted to
understanding and easing it. There are also some
new awesome, low-pressure movements like
No More Lonely Friends, popping up around
the U.S. where you can go to a picnic with
tons of other lonely people! Yay?

NOPE. NOT TODAY, SHIT!
I HEREBY OFFICIALLY RELEASE YOU!
Initials: _____
Date: _____

SHITTY WORRY NO. **31**

I'm Scared to Date

SMALL TALK, WHAT TO WEAR, HOW'S YOUR BREATH? It's a lot. On top of that you need to be charming, funny, interesting, and pay attention to someone else. Oh, and if things go well, look out, because that's when the really big risks start—like opening your heart, mind, body, soul, and closet space to another person. It would be so much easier to just stay single and collect cats.

LET GO OF THAT SHIT!

Everyone who wants love faces the same struggles. Even rock stars get nervous on dates. It's OK to be shy. It can be sexy! In the words of Morrissey, shyness is nice—and shyness can stop you from doing things you'd like to do. (Pro tip for date butterflies: focus on the other person. Ask them questions.)
Scared of heartbreak? Slow down, pardner...
Friendship is awesome and huge.
But remember: cat-collecting is
not cheap. It involves mucho
heartache. Plus poop.

NOPE. NOT TODAY, SHIT!
I HEREBY OFFICIALLY RELEASE YOU!
Initials: _____
Date: _____

I'm Bad at Small Talk

WAITING FOR A MEETING TO START, STANDING AROUND AT A PARTY... daily life demands you to constantly talk without really saying anything. How do some people do it? Are they sorcerors or something? You can stretch a discussion of the weather to five minutes maximum. Then what? If only you could ask interesting questions without seeming like a super creep. Gah! Hot enough for ya?

LET GO OF THAT SHIT!

Hey, we're an awkward species, and we need to awkwardly chat about nothing—all the time, apparently. It's the circle of life! That's why they invented baseball. Just mention baseball, or some equivalent—movies, weekend plans, recent vacations. Or go meta and talk about not being good at small talk!? In any case, remember that the burden is not all on you. Sometimes, just smiling is enough to get other people to get the awkward ball rolling.

NOPE. NOT TODAY, SHIT!

I HEREBY OFFICIALLY RELEASE YOU!

Initials: _____ Date: _____

I'm Afraid to Speak Up When I Want Something

EXPRESSING YOUR DESIRES AND NEEDS should be as easy as falling off a log into a pool of whipped cream, right? When you were little, you had no problem saying what you wanted for your birthday, or for dinner, or to watch on TV. But over the years you've learned the messy truth about saying what you want: It's messy. It leads to conflict! Expectations! Disappointments! Plus, it's like Murphy's Law or something—if you let the Universe know what you want, it's waaay less likely to happen.

LET GO OF THAT SHIT!

You're not passive, you're flexible! Flexible is cool! Side note: Obvs there's a difference between being flexible and denying your own needs and desires. As a human, it's kinda your job to tend to those things (within legal and ethical limits, of course!). The Universe won't punish you—it needs to know what you want. Otherwise, you might get soap-on-a-rope.

NOPE. NOT TODAY, SHIT!

I HEREBY OFFICIALLY RELEASE YOU!

Initials: _____

Date: _____

Um, Is My Body Getting Older?

LATELY YOU'RE STARTING TO WONDER WHOSE BODY YOU'RE IN... because it's different than before. Did it used to be taller? What's with the achiness? What's going on with that situation under your eyes? Your body used to move fast and do amazing things without complaining! And it used to make a lot less popping and clicking sounds when it was doing those amazing things...right? It's kinda hard to remember things.

LET GO OF THAT SHIT!

Good news: You're alive! Because of this, you're also getting a teensy bit less-young all the time. It's kind of a thing that starts in the womb and stops when you die. So, given that admittedly harsh reality, consider this question: What's the alternative to aging? Um, it's *not being alive*. Aging is proof that you're lucky—you're alive and kicking. So feel free to go kick some ass, whatever your age. Hey, 60 is the new 40.

NOPE. NOT TODAY, SHIT!
I HEREBY OFFICIALLY RELEASE YOU!

Initials: _____

Date: _____

SHITTY WORRY NO. **35**

Once I Get to a Certain Point Everything Will Be Perfect

YOUR LIFE ISN'T 100% PERFECT...maybe work's stalled out, you haven't yet met "the One," and spiritual or financial freedom seem utterly out of reach. But someday, once you've crushed your goals...look out! That's when your REAL life's gonna start. You'll be super happy! You'll totally love yourself! You'll finally enjoy each perfect moment of your perfect life!

LET GO OF THAT SHIT!

Psssst. You! Yes, you! Your life is happening RIGHT NOW. Right now while you are holding this (amazing) book in your hands, your life is happening. There is a BEFORE part of your life, which happened liked thirty seconds ago, and a LATER part of your life, which will be happening when you turn the page, and there is a PRESENT part of your life, which is the part you are always living. You are here now. This moment is your real life. HOORAY! Some people are reading terrible books right now.

NOPE. NOT TODAY, SHIT!
I HEREBY OFFICIALLY RELEASE YOU!

Initials: _____

Date: _____

I'm Too Busy for Self-Care

THERE ARE ONLY TWENTY-FOUR HOURS IN A DAY, and you're asleep for part of that time. Then you're busy with your major daily commitments (work, family, school, etc.). If you magically have twenty free minutes, you can't waste it meditating, walking, journaling, yoga-ing, and the like. That stuff's nice, but you're not in the leisurely-stroll phase of life. You're in the takin'-care-of-business, takin'-care-of-other-people phase.

LET GO OF THAT SHIT!

Wait a second, you're reading this book, right? That's a form of self-care right there! If you broaden your definition of self-care, you'll see that you're already doing it. Paying your bills on time is a form of self-care. Not returning your mom's text until you're ready is self-care. Taking a five-minute walk is self-care. Now, think of three more things you already do like this. Take one deep belly breath for each thing you can think of. See, you probably feel better already!

NOPE. NOT TODAY, SHIT!

I HEREBY OFFICIALLY RELEASE YOU!

Initials: _____

Date: _____

I'm a Super-Fraud

YOU'VE COME SO FAR. Yet with each achievement and milestone you rack up, there are still these boring but loud voices in your head: You didn't really earn your accomplishments. You got lucky! They took pity on you. And soon, very soon, you're going to be found out as a fraud!

LET GO OF THAT SHIT!

Fuck those voices. What do they know? Those voices have never had to keep a full-time job, manage relationships, shower, and keep up with the laundry. They have no authority to tell you anything at all, especially about yourself. This may or may not be comforting, but imposter syndrome is universal. (Even former First Lady Michelle Obama says she has it.) So tell the voices to get a life and stay out of yours!

NOPE. NOT TODAY, SHIT!

I HEREBY OFFICIALLY RELEASE YOU!

Initials: _____

Date: _____

I Have to Do to Do Everything Perfectly Perfectly!

ON REALLY GOOD DAYS, you might secretly wonder if, possibly, you could be a genius. (And you might actually BE a genius—for real.) But you also expect genius-level brilliance and technical perfection from yourself…all the time, even with the most inconsequential tasks, like cleaning the floor. And you usually find something to criticize in your efforts, as if you were a contestant on a reality TV floor-cleaning competition. It's exhausting being so brilliant-and-also-human.

LET GO OF THAT SHIT!

Hey, Genius! Guess what? Along with being super brilliant, you are also, um, human. Yeah, sorry about that. You are doing the best you can with what you've got and it has to be said: You are doing a really good job. If there were one area where you could improve though, it might be cutting yourself some much-deserved slack. (See what we did there?) Trust that you are doing your best and are the best. And you do not need to be perfect in all areas, or even one area.

NOPE. NOT TODAY, SHIT!

I HEREBY OFFICIALLY RELEASE YOU!

Initials: _____

Date: _____

SHITTY WORRY | NO. **39**

My Social Feed Confirms It: I'm a Loser!

WHEN YOU'RE STRESSED OR SAD OR HANGRY, it's so, so tempting to go for a nice, "relaxing" scroll. It's soothing to admire people's perfectly curated homes, wardrobes, food, trips...Until a lovely scroll turns into a toxic, depressing spiral. And your reality feels many shabby lightyears from the filtered nirvana of those lucky, beautiful people.

LET GO OF THAT SHIT!

As you totally know (but somehow sometimes always seem to forget?), what we see on social media is basically a bunch of curated highlight reels. People generally only show the very best, most aspirational, most filtered images to their followers. Try "zooming out" on these images and imagine what is happening just outside the frame. That three-tiered birthday cake someone made for a five-year-old? It's awesome, but ten feet away is a counter full of dirty dishes. Oh, and if you peeked in the trash, you'd also find two cakes that failed.

NOPE. NOT TODAY, SHIT!
I HEREBY OFFICIALLY RELEASE YOU!
Initials: _____
Date: _____

I Want to Be Good at Stuff— on the First Try. Dammit.

YOU'RE SPECIAL, AND TALENTED, and you've mastered lots of skills that other people find super difficult. Maybe because of this, you have unusually high expectations of yourself, sometimes expecting near-professional results almost overnight. It's like when you were little and you watched the Olympics...then ran outside thinking you'd be able to do a flip. The difference now is that, as an adult, you're pretty hard on yourself when your attempted flip looks more like awkwardly tripping on your shoelaces.

LET GO OF THAT SHIT!

It's so easy to forget what it's like to learn things. You may be the very best driver you know, but remember how long it took to learn to drive? You had to take classes—for weeks! It's OK for things to take their time to get to you, whether it's results of a test, or a sourdough starter that won't rise, or your next bestseller's release date. Just add patience to your list of special skills superpowers! If you just keep trying, eventually you will get better at anything. Promise.

NOPE. NOT TODAY, SHIT!

I HEREBY OFFICIALLY RELEASE YOU!

Initials: _____

Date: _____

I Suck at Public Speaking

OMG YOU HAVE TO WHAT? IN PUBLIC?! Not gonna happen. There is no way you're going to be able to get up in front of those people and talk out loud. Just thinking about it is making your heart race and your body sweat and your vision go blurry and your mouth dry up like a creekbed in the desert. You'll trip over your words, make bad jokes, space important info, get stuff wrong, and just sound plain stupid. Everyone will laugh at you. There is no way you are going to speak in public ...and survive.

LET GO OF THAT SHIT!

You're right, public speaking is daunting. And that trick of imagining the audience naked is not going to work, because an audience full of naked people is terrifying and gross. But look, everyone there wants to have a good time and wants you to do well. Everyone there has stuff they're worrying about in their lives. Focus on *them* and how you can help them with the information you have to share. Bonus: no matter how badly you do, you will live to tell the tale.

NOPE. NOT TODAY, SHIT!
I HEREBY OFFICIALLY RELEASE YOU!

Initials: _____   Date: _____

I'm Basically Scared of Everything

LET'S SEE... you're afraid of spiders, snakes, public restrooms, the subway, most trains really, flying, spicy food, dying alone, confronting your mother, telling people what you really think, eating a caramel apple, deep water, to-go cups with hot drinks in them, going gray, sewer grates, all flying bugs, elevators, the number 13 and so, so, so much more. Why even bother leaving your house, or even your bed for that matter? It seems like the whole world is out to get you!

LET GO OF THAT SHIT!

There is a whole big, beautiful world out there, and you're missing out. Have you ever heard of someone getting trapped in an elevator, in deep water, while holding a to-go cup with a swarm of cicadas? No. Give yourself a chance to live and find out for yourself how much fun life can be when you're not giving into what very may well be irrational fears.

NOPE. NOT TODAY, SHIT!

I HEREBY OFFICIALLY RELEASE YOU!

Initials: _____ Date: _____

SHITTY
WORRY

NO. **43**

I'm Just
Not That
Interesting

EVERYONE AROUND YOU SEEMS TO BE AN EXPERT HANG GLIDER or a breatharian, or the kind of person who goes to nudist resorts for vacation and here you are: a carb-addicted accountant who can't exist on air alone, whose last vacation was at your mom's house. Boring. Normal. Average. Nothing special at all. Remember that time you were telling your funniest anecdote and the person you were talking to said "I'm sorry, what were you saying?" Yup. That's your life in a nutshell.

LET GO OF THAT SHIT!

Meh. The reason you think you're boring is (probably) not because you're actually boring—it's because you're you. It's all a matter of perspective. If you attended a party in a completely different part of the world, in a completely different environment, people would find you FASCINATING. You would be the least-boring person in the room. Unless like David Bowie was at the same party. In comparison to Bowie, yeah, you're probably boring.

NOPE. NOT TODAY, SHIT!

I HEREBY OFFICIALLY RELEASE YOU!

Initials: _____

Date: _____

I'm Scared of Being an Epic Failure

YOU WANT TO TAKE RISKS—career moves, creative projects, personal challenges and goals. But you're also paralyzed by the fear that you'll do a giant face-plant in front of everyone, and the whole wide world will point and laugh at the sad weirdo flailing on the ground (YOU), who tried to fly and crash-landed for all to see! And a voice will boom from the heavens with a resounding BWAH HA HA, and you'll be ridiculed wherever you go forever...so you better settle for what you've got.

LET GO OF THAT SHIT!

Society sends us some pretty toxic messages about so-called success. It says: Money = Success, and Success = Your Value as a Person. Here's the kicker: Most people who have deathbed regrets say things like, "I wish I had allowed myself to be happy," "I wish I had been true to myself," "I wish I had spent more time with people I love." Not much about "I wish I hadn't tried that thing my soul longed to do." So what if you do a public nosedive? Will you die? Or will life go on, and everyone will forget about it in five minutes?

NOPE. NOT TODAY, SHIT!

I HEREBY OFFICIALLY RELEASE YOU!

Initials: _____

Date: _____

I'm Unloveable

DO YOU FEEL IF PEOPLE ONLY KNEW THE REAL YOU, THEY'D GO RUNNING? If they only knew that you sometimes don't wash your hair for three (or four!) days or that you cheat at board games, and that you have no desire to travel and you don't like to spoon? If they did, they'd discover your big secret: You are basically unloveable.

LET GO OF THAT SHIT!

When you think about the reasons you love others, do travel plans really have all that much to do with it? Or hair-washing habits? (Is that even a thing?) Granted, you may not be a stuffed animal or a platter of hot cheesy garlic bread, but there is SO MUCH about you that is loveable. Your heart. Your spirit. Your weird talent for naming celebrities who look alike. Most, your you-ness. Unlike showering technique, that IS a thing—and it is priceless.

NOPE. NOT TODAY, SHIT!

I HEREBY OFFICIALLY RELEASE YOU!

Initials: _____

Date: _____

Look at That Sh*t Go!